CESR- Leadership Indoctrination

Contents

Dedications: 2
Tags & Legend.. 3
CESR - Leadership Indoctrination Workbook .. 35
    Questions 35
Practical Exercise 63

Dedications:

Thank you, to my Lord and Savior; for giving me the desire and skill-set to accomplish something to help guide others.

Thank you to my Wife, (Crystal Danyel); for the love, patience, and understanding while I spent a great amount of time and effort developing the content of this project.

Thank you to the men & women of the United States Army that I served alongside, who helped develop & shape the leadership skills I stand on today.

Thank you to the Company (Lincoln & Hill); for seeing this project as a viable asset to the mission & vision.

Tags & Legend

Divide-Digital Tag: depicts the differences perceived by access to or /lack of global information

Ex Tag: depicts a person, a place or thing from your past

Hope Tag: depicts a person, a place or thing that provides reassurance or confidence to the hopeless

Audio Commentary tag: depicts a piece of supplementary audio information

CESR- Leadership Indoctrination

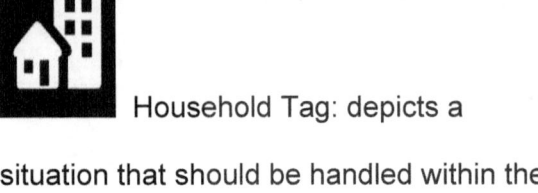 Household Tag: depicts a situation that should be handled within the home

Lighthouse Tag: depicts being a valid example within God's will

Man-Code Tag: depicts unwritten or unspoken thinking, manners or actions held true by male gender even without evidence of validity

Memory Tag: depicts a verse or passage recommended for memorization

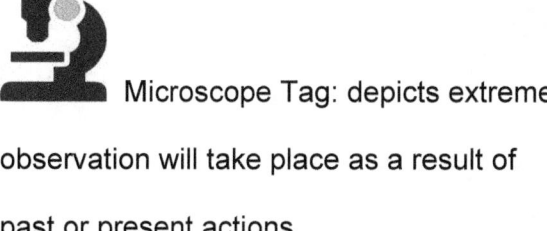 Microscope Tag: depicts extreme observation will take place as a result of past or present actions

 Recharge Tag: depicts a need to refresh your body, mind or spirit

 Resource Tag: depicts a form of information available to supplement a concept

Snooze-U-Lose Tag: depicts slow acting or thinking resulting in opportunities being missed

CESR- Leadership Indoctrination

 Watchman Tag: depicts a person/mentee could be observing how you respond

Argument Tag: depicts a heated exchange of words

Back against the wall Tag: depicts unfavorable circumstances; past, present, and foreseeable future

 Behavior-Illicit Tag: depicts illegal behavior that is tolerance driven

CESR- Leadership Indoctrination

 Behavior-Inherited Tag: depicts behavior that is instinctively driven

 Behavior-Surrounding Tag: depicts behavior that is environmentally driven

 Behavior-Taught Tag: depicts behavior that is learned progressively

 Beyond The Box Tag: depicts behaviors, thoughts, actions outside normal scope of individuals or group

CESR- Leadership Indoctrination

Bird's Eye Tag: depicts a deeper look into a subject surrounding a person, place or thing

Booking Tag: depicts an opportunity to for a speaker is available

Booty Call Tag: depicts a sexual encounter that's counterproductive to relationships

Caught-up Tag: depicts an action that directly resulted in negative circumstances

CESR- Leadership Indoctrination

 Caveat Tag: depicts a specific threat when considering additional information about this subject

Coach Tag: depicts a personal philosophy is available to be learned

 Commentary Tag: depicts supplementary data through public research & discussions that we may oppose or support subject but used for teaching purposes

Content tag: depicts supplementary data through public research

& discussions that we may oppose or support but use for teaching

 Cornerstone Tag: depicts a fundamental principle

Aa Definition Tag: depicts words or phrases that are not considered common

Directional Tag: depicts perceived versus true direction of moral compass

Discipleship Tag: depicts lesson that require a mentor/mentee relationship

Divide-Cultural Tag: depicts the differences perceived by ethnicity

Divide-Economical Tag: depicts the differences perceived by financial assets and net-worth

Divide-Educational Tag: depicts the differences perceived by access to and completion of higher education

Divide-Legal Tag: depicts the differences perceived by interaction with the legal system

 Divide-Racial Tag: depicts the differences perceived by outer physical appearance

End-of-Rope Tag: depicts the end of human strength and the beginning of God's strength

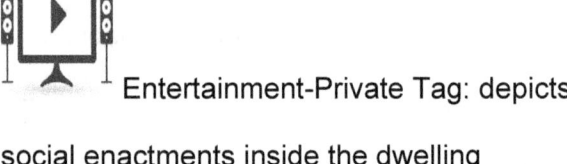 Entertainment-Private Tag: depicts social enactments inside the dwelling

Evangelism Tag: depicts the opportunity to spread the good news

Examine Heart Tag: depicts a circumstance that will harden or soften the heart

Film Tag: depicts supplementary data through developed negative footage to support or refute a philosophy or teaching

Footsteps Ordered Tag: depicts a path inspired by faith of God's will

Forces-Unseen Tag: depicts intangible spiritual opposition

CESR- Leadership Indoctrination

♀ Gender-Female Tag: depicts the actions of a female has transpired

♂ Gender-Male Tag: depicts the actions of a male has transpired

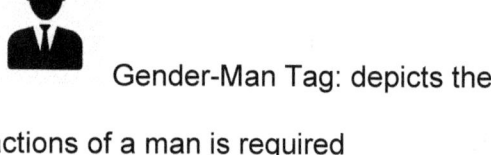 Gender-Man Tag: depicts the actions of a man is required

Gender-Woman Tag: depicts the actions of a woman is required

Healing Tag: depicts a person, a place or thing that can help start the healing process.

Hearing the Word Tag: depicts the individually or corporately heard proclamations of the scriptures

In-a-Hole Tag: depicts a previous choice that has put a person or people in an immoral situation or at a disadvantage

CESR- Leadership Indoctrination

Influenced Tag: depicts the people, places or things that individuals get swayed by

Influencer Tag: depicts the people, places or things that sway other individuals

Inner Struggle Tag: depicts opposing options are available but only one can be selected

Issue-Educational Tag: depicts an issue pertaining to the education system

CESR- Leadership Indoctrination

Read It Tag: depicts a lesson or information that requires reading or learning

LIFE project Tag: depicts principles associated with the training curricula

Love Triangle Tag: depicts 3 people intertwined in 1 connection

Measured Tag: depicts the qualitative or quantitative results of circumstances portrayed or observed

Motivational Tag: depicts more energy is needed to prevail in current circumstances

Nugget Tag: depicts more information can be learned about a person, a place or thing with a desire to dig deeper

Parental Tag: depicts a decision must be made with the best interest of the child/children at its core

Pause Tag: depicts taking a break within a situation to rethink direction before proceeding

CESR- Leadership Indoctrination

Pivot Point Tag: depicts a juncture that the movement required, changes the trajectory permanently

Plan Tag: depicts individuals or a couple have written procedures to follow

Playing the Fool Tag: depicts willingly or unwillingly tolerating the foolishness of others

Positive/Negative Tag: depicts the current situation has a 50/50 potential of going either direction

CESR- Leadership Indoctrination

 Prayer Tag: depicts the need for the power of prayer is imminent

 Prerequisite Tag: depicts requirements prior to starting something

Red Handed Tag: depicts being caught in the act

Replay Tag: depicts the attempt to retry a circumstance from the past to accomplish a different outcome without new skills or information

CESR- Leadership Indoctrination

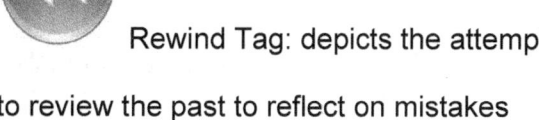 Rewind Tag: depicts the attempt to review the past to reflect on mistakes

 Risk Tag: depicts incorrectly placing faith in chance

 Scripture Tag: depicts a cross-reference to another biblical passage in correct context of meaning

 Skip Tag: depicts the attempt to bypass steps in the process

Sphere-Friendship Tag: depicts the sphere of influence dictated by the associates selected

Sphere-Home Tag: depicts the sphere of influence dictated by parental training

Sphere-World Tag: depicts the sphere of influence dictated by the world

Temptation Tag: depicts a person, a place or things that is a potential hindrance to an objective

Testimony Tag: depicts a former test that requires sharing of a testament of survival

Transferred Knowledge Tag: depicts information shared with the next generation

Under the Radar Tag: depicts a subject that is going unnoticed purposely or unintentionally

Video Tag: depicts supplementary data through digital footage to support or refute a philosophy or teaching

Watchman Tag: depicts a person/mentee could be observing how you behave or respond

Action Time Tag: depicts individuals or a couple must physically move on principle learned

Active Listening Tag: depicts one individual should be actively listening each time another individual is talking in the communication process

Advice Tag: depicts information from confidant for emphasizing key point

Audio Commentary Tag: depicts supplementary data through audio footage to support or refute a philosophy or teaching

Caution Tag: depicts the subject or information should be approached carefully

Challenge Tag: depicts individuals or a couple must complete an assignment immediately before moving to next concept

Championed Tag: depicts a social philosophy that is influencing others positively or negatively

Checkpoint Tag: depicts a location gauge during subject or individual progression

Communicate Tag: depicts general subject matter verbalized between male & female cohorts

Connection Tag: depicts a link to other materials available through the L.I.F.E project

Discussion Tag: depicts specific subject matter verbalized between male & female cohorts

Divide-Political Tag: depicts the differences perceived by political affiliation

Divide-Spiritual Tag: depicts the differences seen based on religious practices

Entertainment-Public Tag: depicts social enactments outside the dwelling

Fast Forward Tag: depicts visualization of the future direction of individuals dictated by actions taken

Woo Tag: depicts attempting to physically or mentally influence an individual temporarily

👁 Forces-Seen Tag: depicts tangible human opposition

 Go back Tag: depicts individuals or a couple is required to review a subject already mentioned

📖 Hermeneutics Nugget Tag: depicts individuals or a couple should further research & study the theological interpretation in a scripturally accurate context

High Priority Tag: depicts critical information or concept in specific session or chapters about a particular subject

Investigate Tag: depicts individuals or a couple should further research & study subject matter

Issue-Financial Tag: depicts an issue pertaining to the economic system

Issue-Judicial Tag: depicts an issue pertaining the justice system

CESR- Leadership Indoctrination

Issue-Political Tag: depicts an issue pertaining to the political process

Issue-Social Tag: depicts an issue pertaining to social injustices

Key Point Tag: depicts main topics covered in specific subject, session or chapter

Practical Exercise Tag: depicts individuals or a couple must complete an assignment before next session can proceed

 Quick Start Tag: depicts an individual or couple addressing a subject or request with first thought (no extra time for contemplating better answer)

Reflection Tag: depicts individuals thinking about subject or questions before providing an answer

Sand of Time Tag: depicts individuals or a couple must make a time sensitive decision to proceed

Beyond The Box Tag: depicts behaviors, thoughts, actions outside normal scope of individuals or group

Change Tag: depicts a personal evolution that is forces or natural

Life Hack Tag: depicts a strategy or technique adopted to manage time and activities more efficiently

Promiscuous Tag: depicts indiscriminate behaviors, thoughts, actions outside the normal scope of relationships

CESR - Leadership Indoctrination Workbook

The questions below reflect some of the most common areas related to any of the CESR – Leadership Indoctrination sessions. Answer all questions. **Discuss & Share** your answers with your cohort to provide understanding for each of your responses. Make additional notes if questions/concern aren't answered immediately, information provided in all sessions will help you get clarification plus provide informational cross-referencing.

Questions

(Generational Divide)

1. In what ways has being born in your generation (based on your birth through a 20-year period) hindering or attributing to your outlook on authority?

(Inner Struggle Tag)

1. Which of the leadership principles creates the most conflict for you?

```
┌─────────────────────────────────┐
│                                 │
│                                 │
│                                 │
└─────────────────────────────────┘
```

(Ex-Tag)

1. Everyone is an Ex-something, what about your life as a leader are you ready to remove or overcome? Be specific

```
┌─────────────────────────────────┐
│                                 │
│                                 │
│                                 │
└─────────────────────────────────┘
```

CESR- Leadership Indoctrination

(Watchman Tag)

1. Are there any young followers (family or non-family) that closely follow or look up to you for leadership? If so, why? Be specific

(Temptation Tag)

1. As a leader, what knocks you off your square, causing you to hurt the influence you earned? Why?

(End of Rope Tag)

1. When you have reached the end of your knowledge, experience or understanding; as a leader, what steps do you take next? Why? Where did you learn those steps if any to get back to a positive authoritative figure?

(Advice Tag)

1. What about being a leader; did you get from others through observation or counsel? What qualified them to advice you? Explain your answer

🏃 (In A Hole Tag)

1. Many communities speak of the inherited attributes plaguing individuals and families, as an aspiring leader or experienced leader what have you reaped positively or negatively from your environment/community? Be specific. If negative characteristics, what would you change?

▣ (Pivot Point Tag)

1. If you (as a leader) have experienced a major shift (pivot) in your philosophy, what caused it and why? Be specific

♟ (Change Tag)

1. What practices or principles have you gotten away from as an aspiring or experienced leader, that you would like to return too or incorporate? Why?

CESR- Leadership Indoctrination

(Examine Heart Tag)

1. What's in your heart, about having a position of leadership that is holding you back or thrusting others backwards (it can be perceived as positive or negative)? Explain your answer

```
                                    
                                    
                                    
```

(Influencer Tag)

1. Are you making the household/workspace you preside over a positive atmosphere for following? If you do not preside over a household/workspace what steps are you taking to contribute to

CESR- Leadership Indoctrination

success of the household/workspace you dwell/work?

◎ (Life Hack Tag)

1. As a leader, how is the relationship between you & your mentor effecting how you lead your family/employees/mentee's in your daily effectiveness? Be specific

CESR- Leadership Indoctrination

👣 (Footsteps Ordered Tag)

1. Do you know your purpose as a leader? What is guiding your thoughts, decisions, and actions? Be specific

2. Follow up, to the previous mentor relationship question, what information about leadership has been transferred to you or you are transferring to others? Be specific

📍 (Checkpoint Tag)

1. As a leader, do you reflect who is influencing, leading or mentoring you in leadership etiquette? Reminder *** Having:

CESR- Leadership Indoctrination

a bad influencer/leader/mentor is as negative as not having an influencer/leader/mentor.

🗝 (Key Points Tag)

1. What are some key lessons you have been introduced to about leadership? List them. Are you willing to share them with others to prevent them from going down a bad path?

CESR- Leadership Indoctrination

 (Communication Tag)

1.　As a leader, do you communicate effectively with your family, employees or mentee's? Explain what and how

 (Sand of Times Tag)

1.　Are you letting society, the media, and other external influencers dictate or sabotage your leadership behavior or interactions with people by being coerced into rash decisions?

2.　As a leader, do you have the philosophy, "it's your right" to abuses the positions of authority (i.e. do as say, not as I do)? Explain why or why not

🎓 (Educational Divide Tag)

1. As an aspiring leader or experience leader, do you believe your current educational qualification, is effecting your ability as a leader (in your family, neighborhood, society, and workplace)? If so, what would make you change your leadership qualifications?

⚐ (Argument Tag)

1. As a leader, are you hot-headed in front of your family/employees/mentee's when its related to strategies for conflict resolution? If not so, what keeps you under control? Be specific

🎲 (Risk Tag)

1. As a leader do you have a predisposition to take risk with your family/employee/mentee's lives? Explain Why? If not, are you afraid to? Explain

📏 (Measured Tag)

1. What is your belief (measurement) of a successful leader or advocate? Explain your answers (we assume your definition of success is a reasonable one)

2. As a leader, what behaviors are you submerging family/employees/mentee's in that you're overlooking the long-term effects (if its perceived to be normal where you live or in society)?

👫 (Parental Tag)

1. If you're leader at work but not at home (or vasa versa), how does one place affect the other? Depending on your response, what are the circumstances surrounding the separate expression of leadership levels? Be specific

✊ (Social Issue Tag)

1. With the deaths of several citizens by the actions of the authoritative figures and the heighten call for retaliation, where do you stand as a leader on social change? Do

CESR- Leadership Indoctrination

your social views negatively affect your profession leadership?

(Behavior Taught Tag)

1. Do you feel equipped to share leadership information or lessons to others in subordinate roles: family, employees or mentee's?

(Influencer Tag)

1.   As a leader, are you monitoring the people gaining influence in/over your family, employees, or mentee's lives? If so, what is your process of staying informed? If not, do you know the influencers effects?

(Directional Tag)

1.   As a leader, where is your moral compass taking your leadership aptitude? If not aware of your direction, where would you like to be heading today?

⚠ **(Caution Tag)**

1. As a leader, are you trying to guide your family, employees or mentee's towards your passions? If so, does it help?

 **(Digital Divide Tag)**

1. Between old-school and new school leadership practice, in your interactions

(with male, female, family or friend) which do you prefer to follow? Explain the thinking behind having two agendas (ways) of dealing with people and changing between the two philosophies.

2. As a leader, are you providing every possible access point (technology) for leadership development for your family, employees, or mentee's? If not, what are your developmental alternatives?

 (Coach Tag)

1. As an aspiring or experienced leader has someone (mentor, colleague, friend, or

CESR- Leadership Indoctrination

family member) been trying to teach you something that you have refused to accept (intentionally or unintentionally)? If so, why have you refused the lesson? Be specific

🖎 (Planning Tag)

1. As a leader, what is the vision for your family, employees or mentee's and the roles the play? Is it written down? If so, who else knows about it? If no one knows their roles, what is keeping you from telling them?

(Content Tag)

1. What information (books, podcast, trainings, influencers etc.) are you honing your leadership aptitude with? What effect does it have on your leadership decisions? Be specific

(Investigate Tag)

1. As a leader, is there any relationships or situations, you should examine deeper before letting your reputation become tarnished by the actions of others?

Explain the circumstances

● (Under the Radar Tag)

1. With the new movement of homosexual and transgender individuals; would addressing the rights and privileges of these individual, create a hidden preconception in your leadership style? If so, would you be able to communicate what they are? If not, would you communicate about this issue publically?

CESR- Leadership Indoctrination

(Championed Tag)

1.   As a leader, will you let the increased championing of questionable societal acceptance dictate a way of leading your family, employees or mentee's to you? Explain your answer

```
┌─────────────────────────────────┐
│                                 │
│                                 │
│                                 │
└─────────────────────────────────┘
```

(Beyond The Box Tag)

1.   As a leader, are you comfortable using the information and techniques to lead your family, employees or mentee's that you've been introduced to, in order to keep them from being boxXxed-in by society?

CESR- Leadership Indoctrination

Explain your answer

[ ]

🯅 (Prayer Tag)

1. As a leader, would you consider allowing private prayer during work hours (even though in most corporations it is forbidden)? Be specific

[ ]

CESR- Leadership Indoctrination

 (Active Listening Tag)

1. Do you have an open door policy for your family, employees or mentee's? If not does it affect your communication?

2. As a leader, do you find yourself listening too or hearing your family, employees or mentee's need? Explain

(Discipleship Tag)

1. Who are your successor(s) and why were they selected? If none, what obstacles as a leader, have prevented from you beginning to train someone your vision? If so, do you have an estimated completion

date? If not, do you have an estimated initiation date? Explain your answers

▪ (Cornerstone Principle Tag)

1. As a leader, what is your fundamental stance? Will your family, employees or mentee's know not to challenge that position?

▪ (Back Against the Wall Tag)

1. As a leader, when you're up against deadlines, attrition or other work related

difficulties what approach do you take towards family, employees or mentee's? Be specific

🔨 (Nugget Tag)

1. What about leadership have you been intrigued to dig deeper into its meaning, to better equip yourself? If you do not have a desire for more leadership development, why not?

🔬 (Microscope Tag)

1. Once you begin to change toward being a standup leader, more eyes will be upon you. As a leader you're already under the microscope (based on your spiritual affiliation, age, race, economical background, and marital status to mention a few) do you have a strategic plan to combat the extra scrutiny when your family, employees or mentee's behavior and actions become socially unacceptable?

Practical Exercise

 Practical Exercise:

Of the categories; as a leader what is the most difficult for you to master? List the problem(s) and other trustworthy and qualified leaders to potentially seek a solution from.

CESR- Leadership Indoctrination

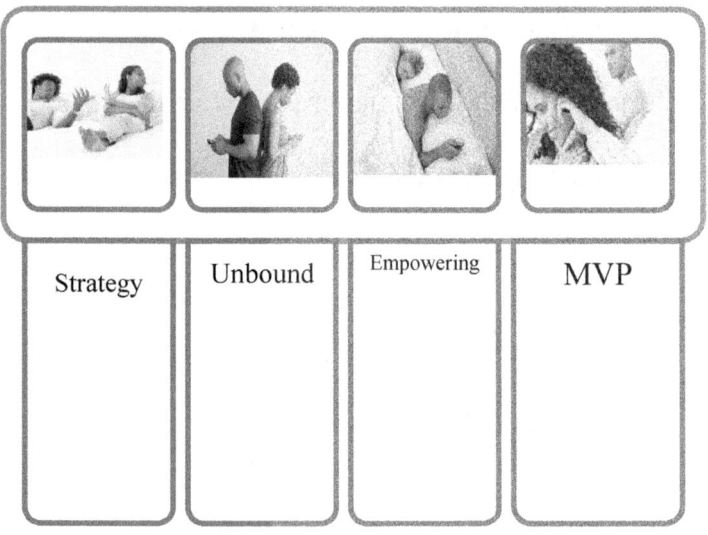

Strategy	Unbound	Empowering	MVP

www.ingramcontent.com/pod-product-compliance
Lightning Source LLC
Chambersburg PA
CBHW061216180526
45170CB00003B/1019